Triceratops

by Wil Mara

Content Consultant
Gregory M. Erickson, PhD
Paleontologist
The Florida State University
Tallahassee, Florida

Reading Consultant
Jeanne Clidas
Reading Specialist

Children's Press®
An Imprint of Scholastic Inc.
New York Toronto London Auckland Sydney
Mexico City New Delhi Hong Kong
Danbury, Connecticut

Library of Congress Cataloging-in-Publication Data
Mara, Wil.
  Triceratops/by Wil Mara.
    p. cm.
  Includes bibliographical references and index.
  ISBN-13: 978-0-531-20862-5 (lib. bdg.) ISBN-10: 0-531-20862-1 (lib. bdg.)
  ISBN-13: 978-0-531-20931-8 (pbk.)   ISBN-10: 0-531-20931-8 (pbk.)
  1. Triceratops—Juvenile literature. I. Title.
  QE862.O65M37 2012
  567.915'8—dc23   2011032560

1 2 3 4 5 6 7 8 9 10 R 21 20 19 18 17 16 15 14 13 12

Photographs © 2012: Black Hills Institute of Geological Research, Inc./Ed Gerken: 28,
29; Getty Images: 20, 31 bottom right (Dave King/Dorling Kindersley), cover (Highlights
for Children/Oxford Scientific); iStockphoto/JoeLena: 26, 27; Media Bakery: 8, 31 top
left; Photo Researchers: 4 (Chris Butler), 24 (Mark Hallett Paleoart), 16, 31 bottom
left (Tom McHugh); Superstock, Inc.: 18 (De Agostini), 14 (Stocktrek Images);
The Image Works: 6, 7, 22, 31 top right (The Natural History Museum), 10, 11
(ullstein bild-histopics).

TABLE OF CONTENTS

THE LAST OF THE DINOSAURS

Triceratops (try-SAYR-ah-tops) was one of the last dinosaurs on Earth. It lived about 65 million years ago.

It ate plants.

It did not eat other animals.

Triceratops had a round plate at the back of its head. This was called a frill.

Triceratops did not live alone.

It liked to live in groups.

A BIG DINO

Triceratops was almost
as long as a school bus.
It was as heavy as a large
elephant.

The head was very large. It was as big as an adult person!

FEEDING TIME

Triceratops ate plants that were near the ground. These were easy to reach.

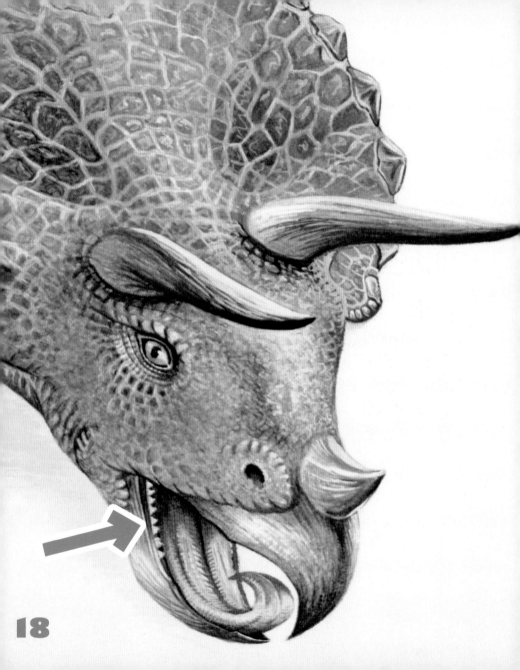

It had hundreds of small teeth. They were in the back of its mouth. It used them to chew its food.

A FIGHTER

Triceratops had three horns on its head.

There was one horn over each eye. Each was as long as your leg!

Hallett '78

The third horn was on the nose. It was smaller than the two eye horns.

Triceratops may have used the horns to fight.

It sometimes fought with Tyrannosaurus rex.

DINOSAUR BONES

Scientist found Triceratops bones. They built a skeleton from the bones. It is in a museum.

Can you find where the three horns are on this skeleton? Can you find the teeth?

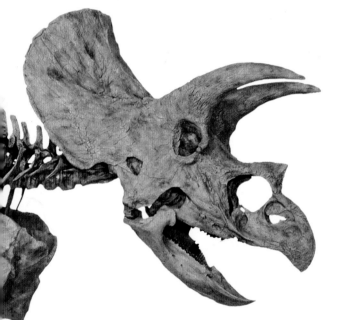

TRY THIS! You might want to explain to your child that scientists have to rebuild dinosaur skeletons from many different pieces, and it takes a lot of careful work. Go back in the book with your child and count the horns on the dinosaurs on page 4. Your child will enjoy finding the corresponding parts of the skeleton in the illustrations and talking about what he just read in the book.

TRICERATOPS FACT FILE

The name Triceratops means "three-horned face."

The Triceratops is the state dinosaur of Wyoming.

Visit this Scholastic web site for more information on the Triceratops: **www.factsfornow.scholastic.com**

WORDS YOU KNOW

frill

horns

plants

Triceratops

Index

Learn More!

You can learn more about the Triceratops at:

www.childrensmuseum.org/ themuseum/dinosphere/profiles/ kelsey.html

About the Author

Wil Mara is the award-winning author of more than 100 books, many of them educational titles for young readers. More information about his work can be found at *www.wilmara.com*.